THE
GHOSTLY TALES
OF
THE
OHIO STATE
REFORMATORY

Published by Arcadia Children's Books
A Division of Arcadia Publishing
Charleston, SC
www.arcadiapublishing.com

Spooky America is a trademark of Arcadia Publishing, Inc.

First published 2021

Manufactured in the United States

ISBN: 978-1-4671-9819-6

Library of Congress Control Number: 2021938345

NOTE: Chapter 4 contains updated information regarding the capture of Frank
Freshwaters which was not included in the original book.

Notice: The information in this book is true and complete to the best of our
knowledge. It is offered without guarantee on the part of the author or Arcadia
Publishing. The author and Arcadia Publishing disclaim all liability in connection with
the use of this book.

All images courtesy of Shutterstock.com; p. 2–3 Sandra Foyt/Shutterstock.com;
p. 30 Mariah97/Shutterstock.com; pp. 52–53, 106–107 ehrlif/Shutterstock.com;
pp. 96–97 arthurgphotography/Shutterstock.com..

Spooky America

THE GHOSTLY TALES OF THE OHIO STATE REFORMATORY

EMMA CARLSON BERNE

Adapted from *The Haunted History of the Ohio State Reformatory* by Sherri Brake

arcadia®
CHILDREN'S BOOKS

OHIO

OHIO STATE REFORMATORY

TABLE OF CONTENTS

Introduction 5

Chapter 1. Bloody Beginnings 11

Chapter 2. The Ghost on Reformatory Road 19

Chapter 3. Life on the Inside 31

Chapter 4. Escapes and Escapades 41

Chapter 5. Seen in the Halls. 55

Chapter 6. All Is Not Well. 83

Chapter 7. Conclusion 103

MAP KEY

1. Mansfield, Ohio
2. Reformatory Road
3. Site of Ohio Soldiers and Sailors Home
4. Ohio State Reformatory

   ❶ West Wing
   ❷ Solitary Confinement
   ❸ Cell Blocks
   ❹ Administration and Warden's Office
   ❺ Warden's Apartment
   ❻ Commisary
   ❼ Yard
   ❽ Dining Hall
   ❾ Hospital
   ❿ High School
   ⓫ Shoe and Print Shops
   ⓬ Furniture Factory

Ohio State Reformatory

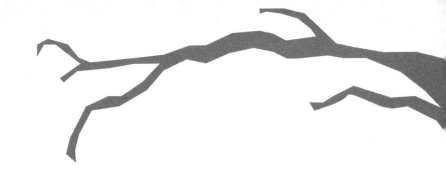

Introduction

The Ohio State Reformatory (often referred to as the OSR) has a dark, foreboding presence that looms above the farm fields of Mansfield, Ohio. With its turrets, towering stone walls, and sprawling grounds, it looks more like a castle than a former prison.

At more than 250,000 square feet (that's the size of five football fields), the reformatory is one of the five largest castle-like buildings in the United States. It is listed in the Guinness Book of World Records for having the largest free-standing

cell block in the world—an impressive six stories tall.

Opened in 1886, over the course of the 104 years it served as a reformatory, the OSR was home to 155,000 prisoners. For the most part, prisons are viewed as places of punishment. But the OSR was built with a different purpose: to motivate prisoners to become better people—to reform them. There was a farm, a print shop, and a shoe

factory, where prisoners could work. And prisoners could take classes in engineering, math, history, and English. There were musical and sports programs.

But the OSR was still a prison. Cell blocks were cramped and crowded. And at night, cell doors clanged shut on the cell blocks and guards patrolled with jingling rings of keys.

As the decades passed, the OSR became less of a reformatory and more of a prison. By 1933, the cell blocks were overflowing with inmates. By 1978, about 2,200 prisoners were being held in one section of the prison meant for 1,200 people.

Because of this, conditions at OSR were brutal and often inhumane. Eventually, the authorities ordered the OSR closed— forever. In December 1990, the last inmates walked out of their cells, bound for the nearby Mansfield Correctional Institute. In 1995, the OSR was turned into a museum for any tourist brave enough to walk the halls and sit for a while in a cell block.

All around, the whispers of the prisoners who lived and died there fill the air. What are they saying? What do they want us to know? What memories lay within the abandoned cells—and what traces did they leave behind?

Bloody Beginnings

Before the OSR existed, the patch of ground where it now sits had its own disturbing history. During the late 1700s and the early 1800s, this area of northeastern Ohio was the site of several bloody battles between Native Americans and early settlers.

As with any fledgling frontier area in early America, Mansfield was troubled by violence, death, and bloodshed. The area was the battleground where Native Americans and settlers clashed as the settlers attempted to make their way west across the land of the indigenous tribes. Raids, massacres, disease, starvation, and loneliness plagued many settlers in this new wilderness. It's safe to say that no one in the area, whether Native American or hopeful settler, was untouched by death. And it may be that some of those who lost their lives never moved on.

Not all settlers who passed through this part of Ohio were wary of the Native Americans in the area. One such notable resident was John Chapman, better known as Johnny Appleseed. He was a bit of an eccentric man, and he made his home in the area now known as Mansfield, Ohio. During his lifetime, he planted thousands of apple trees as he traveled through the area. Johnny Appleseed never married, and he told friends that he believed there would be two spirits in the afterlife who would take care of him if he stayed single while

on earth. It's said that perhaps Johnny Appleseed didn't find those two spirits to look after him, because people claim that he's come back to continue to walk through the apple orchards he planted.

As the years passed, conflicts between Native Americans and settlers became less frequent. But other changes came to the piece of land that would be the home of the OSR.

As the 1860s began, the Civil War split the country in two. Ohio was a Union state, and a training camp for Union soldiers was established near Mansfield. It was named Camp Mordecai Bartley, after the eighth governor of Ohio, and many men lived—and died— on its grounds.

But some of those who were lucky enough to survive battle and their wounds claimed that the camp was haunted, perhaps by those who had died in the area years before.

In 1861, one soldier declared that ghosts and spirits had visited him while he was training. He was so distraught that he couldn't fight anymore, and he was discharged from the army. Two years later, he died in a Kentucky insane asylum.

Soldiers also claimed that their belongings sometimes went missing without explanation. In certain areas of the camp, guns malfunctioned. In the dark shadows of the camp, people heard strange whispers and muffled voices. Sometimes, especially in the northeast corner of the camp, soldiers swore they'd heard voices wafting up from the ground they stood on, as if those who were buried there had one last message to communicate.

The ground that the Ohio State Reformatory would later stand on certainly saw its share of death, disease, and suffering. People who study the paranormal sometimes refer to imprinted energy—energy from the dead that remains in that plot of ground. Perhaps the spirits of the

Native Americans, early settlers, and Union soldiers linger in the area. Perhaps some of the figures lurking in the OSR's abandoned hallways are their spirits, waiting for over a century for someone to notice them.

The Ghost on
Reformatory Road

Over the years, many ghost hunters and
paranormal investigators have visited the
buildings of the OSR. They've walked past
the cells with the gaping doors, the shower
room where rusty stains mar the tiles, the
plaster walls now riddled with damp. Their
footsteps echo through the hospital ward
and the warden's apartment. And many
say that ghosts walk those same paths. The

spirits of the prisoners and the guards rest uneasily within the OSR walls. Sometimes they don't rest at all. Sometimes they reach out.

Not all of the ghosts of the OSR stay within the walls of the prison. Driving up the lonely road to the prison, with your headlights cutting through the darkness

and the black farm fields yawning all around, people say they've sensed the presence of Phoebe Wise—dead for over ninety years but not at peace.

Phoebe Wise was born at some point during the early nineteenth century, one of ten children. Her father was an engineer and a teacher. He brought his family to Mansfield from Baltimore in 1833.

Phoebe loved music. She often played the piano for hours, the notes echoing in the fields around her house late at night. And Phoebe was smart—she loved school and got good grades. Everyone in Mansfield knew that Phoebe Wise was a bright student.

When Phoebe was still a child, her family sold their farm and moved to a new section of land—just north of what would later become the OSR. And there she grew up, reading poetry, playing the piano, and continuing her studies.

In 1887, Phoebe's father died. Four years later, her mother died. Several of Phoebe's brothers and sisters died, too. Soon, only five of the ten children, including Phoebe, were alive.

Phoebe's siblings drifted away from the farm as the years passed, and eventually, Phoebe was all alone. And that's when she started to behave strangely. She would walk with her two dogs and her horse, talking to them. She hardly ever took baths. Her clothes grew odder and odder—she wore old dresses, sometimes several at a time, and crazy hats. The people of Mansfield even had a rhyme about Phoebe:

The children laughed at Phoebe Wise
When she came into town
Wearing a faded bridal veil
And tattered wedding gown.
Her finger bore no marriage ring
A horse slept by her bed
It reared at strangers as they passed
And snorted till they fled.
Oh, Phoebe was peculiar
As daft as a loon
But 'till you've heard her story
Never judge a gal too soon.

But Mansfield did judge Phoebe. The local boys made fun of her, teasing and taunting her when she came into town. People gossiped, speculating that she had inherited a huge amount of money from a relative.

Phoebe's house didn't look like that of a secretly rich woman. Her roof was leaking. The back part of her house was falling in . . . and she seemed to be falling apart, too. She'd always been a gorgeous woman with straight black hair and high cheekbones. But as she aged, like her house, Phoebe was falling into disarray too, wearing torn, dirty men's clothing.

Still, the rumors about Phoebe's secret money persisted in Mansfield. She had money and jewelry hidden in that falling-apart house, people said. And on December 23, 1891, three men broke into her front sitting room. One man grabbed Phoebe and growled at her to tell them where the money was.

Phoebe was old, but she was still smart. She pretended to lead the men to her valuables, but instead, she hoped to snatch her gun.

The men saw what she was trying to do. They tied her up and threatened to kill her unless she told them where her treasures were. Phoebe told them where to find a diamond ring and $500 in cash. The men grabbed the ring and the money and took off.

But Phoebe wasn't going to just lie there. After the men left, she wriggled free of her bindings and made her way to the OSR, where they telegraphed for the police.

The police fanned out looking for the burglars. Soon, they arrested Thomas Bloor, William Tyler, and Henry Zwefel. Henry was the leader of the three and the most experienced criminal. He had already served three years for burglary. All three men were jailed.

Phoebe became famous after this incident. Newspapers all over the county wrote about the break-in and her escape,

and Phoebe was not allowed to live quietly in the peace she so obviously wanted. Instead, a man named Jacob Kastanowitz began stalking Phoebe after reading about her in the papers. He followed her when she came into town. He banged on the door of her home over and over, begging to be let in, pleading that he just wanted to sit with her.

On May 22, 1898, Phoebe lost her temper. When Jacob knocked on the door and declared, "Marry me or kill me," Phoebe snapped. She grabbed her rifle and shot him in the chest. Phoebe was never arrested or charged in Jacob's death. Maybe the authorities agreed with the headline of the local newspaper, which read, "Phoebe Wise Rids Herself of an Intolerable Nuisance."

Phoebe Wise lived another forty-five years, sealing herself up in her falling-down house. Her house was robbed again. The world must have seemed an even more dangerous place to Phoebe after that because she went out less and less. "The Hermit of the Heights," the town called her. Sometimes people saw her walking the perimeter of her property, dressed in filthy clothes and holding her rifle. No one was going to bother Phoebe Wise again. Not if she had anything to say about it.

Phoebe Wise died on March 3, 1933. The townspeople claim that the spring on her property went dry on the very day of her death.

Even in death, Phoebe had no peace. In the days after her funeral, several people broke into her house to look for the treasure still rumored to be within those walls. No one could find it. Phoebe would undoubtedly be angry at these intrusions. All she wanted was to be left alone.

And it appears that Phoebe is still angry at those who harassed and hurt her and wouldn't let her live in peace. People say you can see her at night, her ghostly form walking along Reformatory Road in front of the prison. She still wears her ragged clothing and a frumpy hat, carrying something in the crook of her arm. Are you brave enough to get close enough to see what she's carrying? It could just be a basket, but then again, it could be her rifle . . .

Cell block in the Ohio State Reformatory

Life on the Inside

Early in human history, most societies and cultures practiced justice on a personal or family level. Taking revenge on someone and the practice of "an eye for an eye" were considered justice. As time went on, society moved toward more formal systems of justice based on written codes and a more orderly way of handing out punishment.

As people organized into groups such as larger tribes, villages, and communities, those groups became responsible for the

punishment of criminals. Punishments could be very brutal—from being boiled in oil or burned at the stake, to being hanged by the wrists while being poked by sticks or being fed to wild beasts. And once people began to write, they created lists of crimes and the punishments that went with them.

Once crimes and punishments were written down, courts were established to officially try and sentence criminals. Even though people were no longer fed to wild animals, the punishments could still be quite harsh: branding, flogging, being put into stocks, tar and feathering, and hard labor. (For some criminals, punishment was being sent to a colony to work.) But most people who had been convicted of a crime were put in the local lockup or jail.

While villages, towns, and small communities often had their own jails, it wasn't until the late eighteenth century that the modern prison was developed. At that time, it was thought that prisoners were treated too severely and jails only emphasized strict discipline and hard labor. They were also unsanitary places that caused widespread disease, and men, women, and even children were very often held in the same cells.

Thankfully, changes in attitudes eventually led to changes in laws, and the criminal justice system began becoming more fair. Prisons changed from places where prisoners very often just waited to die, to places of rehabilitation that provided medical care and education. And when the OSR opened in 1896, instead of punishing prisoners, it was hoping to reform them, which means to help them learn and grow to be better people. The building itself had been designed to be an uplifting, inspiring, and intimidating structure. Prisoners were to receive three things during their time at OSR: religion, education, and a trade. (A trade is a skill someone can use to get a job, like learning to be a carpenter or a tailor or an electrician.)

At one time, there were over 1,600 men and boys who were students at the OSR, learning subjects such as math, reading, English, economics, history, and geography. Inmates also learned various trades and worked in the workshops on the grounds, where they learned to run printing presses and made shoes, clothing,

furniture, and machines. Inmates were also involved in building roads and other local improvement projects. Some of the inmates were employed at the farm dormitory and had duties at the poultry farm, dairy, and hog barns. The prison was never fully self-sufficient, but by the early 1930s, prisoners grew and raised most of their own food.

If an inmate became ill during his sentence, he would visit the onsite hospital. The hospital had ninety beds and a full staff of doctors and nurses. One of most serious illnesses that staff and inmates at OSR feared was tuberculosis (or TB). TB is highly contagious and spreads through the air, and early on, there was no cure. At the OSR, TB deaths were high due to the close quarters and how easily and quickly the disease spread. So the TB ward was very often overflowing with patients. The death toll began to fall as living standards improved, and by the 1940s, effective medicines were developed to treat the disease.

The OSR also had its own cemetery. There are over 200 numbered headstones that were placed there as inmates died of old age, disease, or illness. Inmates buried in the cemetery also included those who committed suicide, were murdered, or not claimed by their family.

Life at the OSR changed through the years depending on the type of inmates who were sent there. Originally, it was home to "middle-of-the-road" criminals and those who needed guidance. But as the years passed, more and more hardened criminals were sent to the OSR. For the first forty years (1896 to 1936), the reformatory was cited as one of the best institutions of its kind in the United States. However, this changed in the 1930s when overcrowding became an issue and conditions started to decline. This reached its height in 1978. Then a group of churches and civic groups filed a lawsuit on behalf of the inmates. The group claimed that the prisoners' constitutional rights were being violated. The lawsuit was resolved in 1983, when prison officials

agreed to improve conditions while pre-
paring to close all the cell blocks by the end
of 1986. In 1987, the building was listed in
the National Register of Historic Places.
And in December 1990, the last inmates and
members of staff moved to the Mansfield
Correctional Institute. After ninety-four
years of operation, the massive, castle-like
structure would cease operating. But the
stories of the approximately 155,000 men
and boys who passed through its gates all
left a story—and perhaps a ghost—behind.

Escapes and Escapades

Even though it was called a "reformatory," the OSR was still a prison. And there were prisoners who didn't want to be there or felt that they didn't need to be there to be reformed. Because of that, many prisoners tried to break out of the OSR over the decades. There are prisoners who managed to escape the walls and were never found, and there are some who fled and came back to free other inmates. And more often than not, there are those who escaped and were found and ended up serving all their time at the OSR.

Rarely is a prisoner escape funny, but that was the case with one inmate who decided to get creative about breaking out of the OSR. This inmate apparently convinced other inmates to help him in his attempt. Why they decided to help him without asking to join him in his attempt is unclear. Nevertheless, this crafty prisoner asked his fellow prisoners to nail him inside a crate that was being shipped out of the OSR. The crate was full of shoes that had been manufactured at the reformatory's shoe factory. The shoe factory shipped shoes to various state agencies and other organizations. The prisoner obviously thought that at some point during the shipping process, he would get the chance to break out of the crate and make a quick getaway. However, the inmate's plan was short-lived. The crate of shoes, with the inmate inside, was transported along a highway to Columbus, Ohio. After the truck stopped and it had been quiet for a while, the inmate kicked open the crate. Imagine his surprise when he discovered that his creative escape had landed him at the Ohio State Penitentiary! He had traded his cell at the reformatory for a cell at the penitentiary. This was obviously not the kind of escape he had been hoping for . . .

Some attempts at freedom ended as quickly as they began. And unfortunately for Rudolph Kervinak, who had been convicted of grand larceny and sentenced to do time at OSR, that's exactly what happened. While traveling by train to the OSR with his escort, Sheriff Robert Wells, the eighteen-year-old prisoner escaped by jumping out a window. Sheriff Wells got off the train and found a horse and buggy. He took off in search of the escaped prisoner, alerting townspeople of the fugitive as he rode across the countryside. When he got to Lucas, Ohio, a train operator there told the sheriff that he had seen a man following Kervinak's description skulking through the local graveyard. When officers searched the cemetery, they found the prisoner asleep in a fenced corner. His arms and wrists were badly bruised and swollen, and he was still wearing handcuffs. Sheriff Wells took charge of the prisoner again, and they got back on a train to the OSR. This time Sheriff Wells took no chances and sat very close to his prisoner on the last leg of their journey.

Attempts to get out of OSR happened very soon after the reformatory opened. In November 1902, just eight years after the OSR "welcomed" its first prisoners, an escape occurred involving inmate John Gagnon. Once he managed to put the formidable walls of the prison behind him, Gagnon made his way into nearby Mansfield. Once there, he snuck into Engine

House No. 2 at the local fire department. Some of the firemen caught sight of Gagnon in his gray prisoner clothing and thought he looked suspicious. They started to chase Gagnon but decided perhaps that wasn't a good idea since he might be armed and dangerous. Instead, they called the OSR and local law enforcement and told them of the escaped inmate. As officers tracked Gagnon, they came across a camp of homeless men about four miles from town. And there they discovered Gagnon's discarded prison uniform. Apparently, Gagnon had some outside help, and he had a friend hide clothing for him in a hollow log. The search continued, but Gagnon was never found. He is one of the rare instances of a successful escape from the OSR.

For the few inmates who made successful escapes, there were hundreds who had a chance every day to walk off from their captivity but chose not to. There were hundreds of boys and men at OSR who worked at the reformatory's five "honor camps" that surrounded the outside walls. These inmates were trusted to live in dormitories while being supervised by unarmed guards. Many were not fenced in and not watched for anywhere from a few minutes to nearly an hour. Rarely did an unguarded inmate at an honor

camp attempt to escape. A mainline train ran next to the camps, and jumping on a slow-moving freight train would have been an easy method of disappearing. Why weren't the inmates in these camps tempted to escape? Perhaps because working in an honor camp gave the inmates certain privileges during their free time. They were allowed to play cards, baseball, volleyball, and tennis as a reward for a hard day's work. Life in an honor camp was better than life behind bars—and may have even been better than life on the outside.

But there was one prisoner who decided that even life at an honor camp was too much to endure. At the age of twenty-one, Frank Freshwaters pled guilty to voluntary manslaughter stemming from a 1957 car accident. He initially got probation, but after violating his parole, he was sentenced up to twenty years at the OSR in 1959. Freshwaters earned the trust of the OSR prison officials, and he was given a transfer to an honor farm. After only seven months at the honor farm, Freshwaters escaped—

and authorities have never revealed just how he managed to do it. But in 2015, fifty-six years after walking away from the honor camp,

Frank Freshwaters, who became known as the "Shawshank Fugitive," was finally apprehended in Florida. In February 2016, he was granted parole. Freshwaters was one of Ohio's most wanted criminals and the longest capture in the history of the US marshals.

Cell block in the Ohio State Reformatory

Seen in the Halls

Why would a place like the OSR have ghosts? Anyone who is well versed in paranormal activity knows exactly why. Those who die peacefully, whose souls are not troubled, have no reason to be restless. But those who have endured time in prison, and who may have died there, may have uneasy souls. It is widely believed by prisoners that if you die in prison, your soul remains in prison. And within the walls of the OSR, the restless spirits of its prisoners are said to remain, still confined, locked up for all eternity.

The ghost hunters who visit the OSR usually bring various devices with them. Often they'll come armed with an electromagnetic field meter (EMF) to measure whether electromagnetic fields are low or high in an area. A low reading means that a ghost hunter really might be seeing and hearing a spirit, as opposed to just imagining it. A good ghost hunter might also bring video cameras, digital cameras, and audio voice recorders. Audio recorders are especially important, as ghost hunters use them to record electronic voice phenomena (EVP), the sounds that ghosts and spirits make when trying to communicate with the living. Some use dowsing rods—sticks that sense the presence of ghosts and will cross or move on their own when a ghost is near.

Ghost hunters swear that they've seen black masses floating in the air at the OSR. They've seen white mists and shadowy figures that dart in and out of cells. Glowing balls of light, called orbs, sometimes hover in the air, and sometimes people feel soft fingers stroking or tugging their hair. When they turn around, no one is there. The ghost hunters have moved through strange spots of cold air in rooms that are warm. (Ghosts are often said to be accompanied by unexplained shifts in temperature or pockets of cold air.) Pipe smoke sometimes hovers in the warden's apartment, though no one has smoked inside the OSR since the day its doors were closed. Sometimes, the ghosts turn angry. Visitors have been pushed, shoved, and slapped—but not by any visible form.

Sylvia Triesel visited the reformatory for the very first time in August 2009. While sitting on a bench in the middle of a room in the west wing, she saw what looked like a black shadow peeking out of a cell. Sylvia

thought the form looked like the upper chest, shoulder, and head of a person. The shadow leaned out, went back in the cell, leaned out again, and then disappeared. Sylvia snapped a photo as quickly as she could, hoping to capture the shadow. But when she looked at the picture, there was nothing there. At least there was no living person in the cell . . .

Sheena Marie Harless came from West Virginia for her first ghost hunt at the OSR in 2009. She hoped to experience something unusual that night—and she was not disappointed. Sheena and two other visitors were in a room using EMF meters, but they weren't showing any activity. But as Sheena and the other two guests started speaking, the EMFs went off. When they asked whatever spirits might be around if they wanted the visitors to leave the room, the meters spiked. Sheena felt it was no coincidence that the meters went off. She knew that whatever presence was in the room wanted to be left alone—and Sheena and the other visitors decided to honor that request.

When ghost hunter Bill Wilson began to explore the OSR, he saw someone he calls "the Shadow Man." The Shadow Man appears in the commissary and in the shower room. He wanders in and out of cells, and he doesn't just appear at night— Bill has seen him in daylight too.

Shadowy figures have shown themselves to other ghost hunters too. An investigator named Jared Fischer was leading a group of visitors through the OSR at night. As his flashlight bobbed through the darkness, the group heard loud footsteps tapping at the far end of the cell block. Jared swung around, his flashlight beam cutting through the black. But no one was there.

Jared and the ghost hunters walked on, making their way to another cell block. Jared stopped short and gasped. The entire left side of his body felt as if it had been dipped in ice water. He was so cold, he started to go numb. But everyone else felt fine. There was no draft. No reason for the chill. Soon after, Jared saw something. It was a figure—a human figure—running up the stairs to the third floor. And it wasn't another ghost hunter . . .

Ghost hunter Justin Fink was also visited by the spirits at the OSR on his very first trip. He remembers a soft touch on his arm as he was walking down a hall near the warden's quarters. It wasn't the breeze. No windows were open. And it wasn't a draft. The air outside that night was still.

Justin and his friend Joey walked on, trying not to let the prickles crawl up their backs. But then something else happened, this time on the stair landing. As the two men passed the window on the landing, the pane of glass suddenly shifted with a loud *clunk*. Justin's pulse shot up. "Joey, you touch that?" he asked.

"No, I didn't." Joey shook his head vehemently.

Justin touched the glass. Although it was loose in the frame, it was heavy—about a quarter of an inch thick. There was no way Joey could have stirred up enough air to move it just by walking past. Maybe it was just the old building settling? Possibly. Walls and floors shifted all the time in the OSR. Or could the ghost of a long dead prisoner or guard have shifted it? Justin and Joey didn't know. But they didn't wait around on the landing to find out.

Later that night, Justin was exploring the warden's apartment. He had his audio recorder out. Suddenly, a voice spoke. "You shouldn't be here," a man said. Did he mean Justin? Justin shouldn't be there? The ghost did not speak again.

Later that night, Justin captured a woman's voice speaking from the darkness on his audio recorder. "I'm here," she said. To whom was she speaking? Her long-dead husband? Justin himself? What did she want?

The voices were back the next time Justin visited. He remembers standing with a group near a tunnel and taking pictures. His recorder was on. Later, when he listened back, he heard a wild laugh recorded at the moment he'd been near the tunnels. But when he asked the group later, no one else remembered hearing it.

Cheyrl Kneram has worked at the OSR as a ghost hunt volunteer and tour guide since 2001. One night, she was standing outside the warden's office. She had her voice recorder turned on. Cheyrl's son Matt— also a volunteer—was there, too. They were standing only about a foot apart, waiting and listening. Suddenly, someone gasped— but it wasn't Cheyrl or Matt. Deep, gasping breaths came again and again, as if someone was having trouble breathing. There was no one around them at the time—no one living, that is . . .

Cheyrl admits that she believes in the paranormal but is still somewhat of a skeptic. And the things she sees and hears at the OSR don't really rattle her. But that doesn't go for some of the visitors Cheyrl has led through the OSR. She recalls a group of young men running from the west cell block area after seeing an apparition. "I have seen people run out of the building and leave after having things happen; this is not uncommon," Cheyrl says with a chuckle.

Denise Drake is a believer in the paranormal and has visited the OSR numerous times. She had come during the daytime and toured the empty cells and hallways, learning the history of the massive castle-like structure and what happened behind the walls. She found all of this very interesting, but when she discovered the OSR was hosting overnight ghost hunts, she decided she couldn't pass that up.

Denise's first overnight visit was in November 2003. She and a friend climbed up to the fifth level of cells. Just as Denise's friend said, "Well, I don't feel or sense anything up here," Denise got a freezing cold blast of air on her neck. There were no open windows or doorways nearby. Nothing to explain a sudden draft of cold air. Nothing except the presence of a ghost who wanted to be noticed.

Denise and her friend still wanted to explore. They made their way down to the lower levels where the solitary confinement cells stood. In a long, narrow hallway, the metal doors stood open one after another. The doors were solid sheets of steel with only a tiny hatch for the prisoners to look through.

Each door stood on a sliding metal track. As is closed, it screeched and then slammed with a *thunk*, blocking out the world. Each cell was a cave of blackness. Denise shone her flashlight at one of the cells and then froze. A large black mass stood at the door. Was it the spirit of a prisoner who had been locked away in there?

Denise swallowed. She was getting a feeling from the spirit: anger and rage. Whatever this thing was, it did not want Denise or her friend there.

They left, their hearts pounding. They weren't going to try to make their way into the cell. Not with that *thing* standing there at the doorway.

But Denise's night at the OSR wasn't yet over. She and her friend climbed the stairs out of the solitary confinement area. They stopped to rest on the third tier of the cell block. Denise's friend looked over the map, deciding where they should go next. While she waited, Denise got out her camera. She'd take a couple of shots of the long, dark hallway with the cells lining one side.

Denise raised her camera and just as she did, she saw something out of the corner of her eye. Slowly, she turned. Hands. Two hands, cut off just below the elbows, floated in the cell just to her right. Nothing near them. Nothing else around them. And they were glowing—a strange greenish-blue. Then they disappeared.

Denise whirled around. Her friend was studying his map. He hadn't witnessed this eerie apparition. Denise raised her camera and inched forward. The hands were back. And they'd moved. Now they were at the front of the cell. Denise grabbed her friend and ran. She made sure she didn't look back. If the hands were following them, she didn't want to know.

Like Denise, Shawna Rutter believed in ghosts and was a frequent visitor to the OSR. And even when she had some very spooky things happen, she continued to make trips to the prison. Shawna often felt as if she were being followed and watched as she walked the silent halls at night. Often, she saw orbs—the large spheres of floating light—drifting through the still air.

One night in the east wing shower room, Shawna was using dowsing rods to draw out spirits. These sticks move and cross on their own when the presence of spirits is near. Shawna sensed a spirit nearby. She asked him to show himself. And just then, a large shadow passed across the wall in front of her. Suddenly, the dowsing rods trembled— and crossed. Shawna had not made the movement. They'd moved on their own.

Shawna knew the spirit was near. She wasn't afraid. She stayed quietly with the spirit for a while and then called out that she had to go. Shawna asked the spirit to make a noise for her. Just then, a large piece of plaster fell right at their feet. Dropped off the ceiling? Or thrown by the ghost? Shawna didn't wait to find out. She ran.

Lee Runkle, a volunteer tour guide at OSR, would understand Shawna's experiences. She's seen spirits and apparitions in the OSR as well. When she was leading a large tour group, Lee turned around to see someone breaking off and going into the toilet room nearby. One of the visitors? They were supposed to stay together. Lee hurried into the toilet room to retrieve the wandering visitor and bring him or her back. But there was no one there, though Lee looked in every corner.

The OSR wasn't done with Lee though. Later that day, she found herself in a room with several other volunteers. They were all using their EMF meters, cameras, and recorders to detect spirits. Suddenly, the EMF meters began going off. Cameras were powering down on their own. What was happening? Then the heavy wooden door began rattling in its frame on its own, as if someone was shaking it. Lee and the other volunteers didn't know if someone or something was trying to get in or out . . .

Another time, a friend came to visit Lee, and she decided to take him on a private tour of the OSR. The friend was eager to shoot some video, so Lee took him up to the top of one of the cell blocks. The friend turned on his camera and began shooting down the hallway, then left and right. He wanted to make sure he captured the whole area.

The next day, Lee and her friend sat down to check out the video. They hadn't seen anything strange when they were filming, so they didn't expect to see anything strange on the video. But as the video began, something flitted into the frame. It was running across the floor. It was too small to be a human, but it wasn't an animal. What was it, and why did it want to make itself known?

Aaron is another ghost hunter who has also had spirits reach out to him at OSR. One night in August, Aaron was on a nighttime tour of the prison. He'd walked the halls of the administration wing all evening with forty-two other people. But the rest of the group had decided to head home and Aaron was on his own. Aaron wasn't *completely* alone though, there were two other people in the building. But they were floors below, down in the kitchens and solitary confinement cells.

Aaron felt alone though. The air was still and pressed in around him. He flicked on his night vision video recorder. He swung it around the room and called out to see if any spirits might answer.

Suddenly, Aaron heard someone or something rapping on one of the windows.

He remembered that another ghost hunter had told him that spirits in that area often tapped on windows to get people's attention.

Aaron paused and gathered his courage. The rap came again. The spirit wanted him to notice. If he didn't acknowledge it, what would it do? Aaron didn't want to find out. "Is that you making that noise?" he asked the empty room. A pause. Then a third rap. The spirit was answering.

Aaron was utterly alone in the administration wing—except for whatever was tapping—and he needed to get out. Now. He started backing out of the room, not wanting to turn around.

But in the doorway, Aaron paused. Maybe he was leaving too soon. He had come to hunt ghosts, and it looked like he had found one. Out loud, he asked the spirit to communicate one last time. Nothing. Aaron edged into a stairwell with a window. Again, he asked the spirit to do something. "Come on!" he yelled.

And that was when the spirit answered with a bang on the window so hard, Aaron expected the glass to shatter. He'd heard enough. Aaron fled, running down the darkened hallways until he was out of the administration wing and free of the spirit at the window—at least, he hoped.

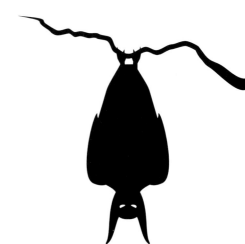

Leann Check and her husband, Dave, are keen ghost hunters who regularly make the one-hour drive from their house to the OSR. Leann calls herself a "sensitive"—she's part of a group of people who feel they can see or feel things that others can't. But Leann's special skills also make the OSR a uniquely frightening place.

The feelings of dread and sadness usually start when Leann is in the shower room. Is she sensing the emotions of the long-dead prisoners who lived and died there? Sometimes the feelings are so overpowering that Leann almost can't bear it. She feels faint and is covered in sweat. Tears well up inside her.

Sometimes the ghosts in the OSR try to communicate with Leann more directly. Once, she was in a room with several others, trying to sense spirits. Suddenly, something hard hit her on the back of the leg. Leann screamed. Something thudded to the floor

behind her. Quickly, one of her friends switched on his flashlight. A small piece of wood lay at Leann's feet. Had she just stumbled into it? Or had a spirit thrown it?

Leann never got an answer. But when she and Dave got home, they inspected the photos of the room they had taken earlier in the evening. There was no wood anywhere in the room. Where had the piece of wood come from? And who threw it? Was the ghost of a long dead prisoner trying to communicate with Leann? Or was it trying to tell her to get out?

These are just a few of the many stories about strange and eerie things that have occurred inside the walls and on the grounds of the OSR. And no doubt there will be many more creepy and spooky happenings there. if you're brave enough, perhaps you could pay a visit to the OSR and add your story to the long list.

All Is Not Well

What *is* a ghost? This is a question those who believe in the paranormal often ask. The answer can be different from person to person. But many believe that a ghost is a spirit who is bound to the earthly world and is not able to go wherever spirits go once their earthly bodies are finished. The spirits don't know that they've died. They're confused—or angry. They stay in the place where they died, and they might try to communicate with anyone nearby.

So what do the ghosts and spirits think about the ghost hunters that invade the OSR every night? The prison walls are their home. Do they welcome investigators poking into the corners and shining flashlights into cells? Or do they want the living out—is the OSR reserved now for the land of the dead? No one knows for sure, of course. But many ghost hunters report that spirits have thrown objects at them or even attacked them. Are these uneasy presences angry at what happened during their lives? Or are they angry at what is happening now, after they are dead?

Ghost hunters have long said that a sudden, violent death is one reason a soul or spirit might remain on earth after the body is gone. This is called imprinted energy. It is said that sometimes the ghost stays behind to warn the living—or to seek revenge on those who dare to approach them.

Jill Keppler started working as a volunteer and tour guide at OSR in 2005. She was first attracted by the magnificent building itself. But soon, the shadows and spirits within its walls drew her further in. The ghosts are everywhere, Jill says. Voices echo from the walls. The spirits of prisoners run in and out of cells. In the warden's office, a blackish ball formed in the doorway in front of Jill's eyes. It flew across the room, and before Jill could react, it hit her. An electric shock ran through her body.

That wasn't the only time spirits turned on Jill in the OSR. One night in November 2009, Jill remembers that she was on the ground floor of the administrative section. A dark shadow came down the stairs. A ghost? A spirit? Friendly—or not? Often, ghosts seem not to notice those watching them. But this one was different.

It turned and walked straight toward Jill. Fear shot through her body. What did the ghost want? What did it intend to do? Jill started praying. The ghost looked at her and then drew closer. Prayers were not enough. Jill touched the cross necklace she was wearing. The ghost stopped. He didn't try to come any further. Jill wasn't sure if it was that action that stopped the menacing spirit in its tracks; she was just glad it stopped.

Some ghosts do go further, as Scott Sukel knows. In 2005, Scott was leading a group of guests through the halls of the OSR at 4:30 in the morning. So far, no ghosts had shown

themselves. Scott and his group wandered up to the third floor of the administration section. The guests scattered to investigate other rooms, and Scott suddenly found himself alone.

Then, pain radiated through his side. It was as if an unseen hand had punched him. Scott dropped to his knees, clutching his side. He looked around wildly. What was it? A vengeful ghost? This was the first time that Scott had ever experienced any kind of hostile activity at OSR. His thinking quickly switched from showing guests around the rest of the building to figuring out how to get everyone out without anyone else being attacked. Trying to not alarm anyone, Scott gathered up the guests and led them out of the OSR.

Scott got home just as dawn was breaking. In the safety of his own house, he lifted his shirt. He gasped. A blue-purple bruise the size of a fist had formed on his side.

After a few days, the bruise faded. But Scott's memories of the angry ghost in the OSR never did.

Laura Lyn had no intention of running during her OSR explorations. Laura is a psychic and she was eager to communicate with the troubled spirits haunting the OSR. One night, one of the OSR volunteers, named Tina, asked Laura for a special favor. There was a spirit haunting one of the bathrooms. Could Laura try to communicate with him?

Laura said she'd try. She made her way up a small, dark stairwell that led to the bathroom. There he was: the entity was a large, dirty-looking man in his thirties. He knew Laura was there. He saw her. Then he screamed obscene names at her and made rude gestures. This spirit was furious.

Laura was shaken. But she stayed where she was. She tried to reason with the ghost, but he warned her, "We will do battle if you do not get out of here."

Laura knew this entity meant business, and she fled. Her palms were sweaty, and her knees shook as she ran down the dark staircase to the office area where the other ghost hunters were waiting. They crowded around as she tried to catch her breath. When she told them what had happened, they wanted to go back with her and see the spirit for themselves.

And then Laura made a mistake. Her instincts as a psychic were telling her not to go back. That spirit was dangerous. He was angry. There was no telling what he might do.

But the other ghost hunters were eager to see him. Laura was a little smug that she had communicated with him. She wanted to show off—just a little. So rather than following her instincts, she led the others to back to the bathroom.

Then, as they crept into the dark bathroom, Laura stumbled. She caught herself, regained her balance—and then something pushed her hard in the back. It was almost as if someone heavy were falling on her. Then the force increased—she was violently shoved. Laura fell so hard that she broke the porcelain floor and cut her hands and knees.

Laura scrambled to her feet, trying to catch her breath. "Come out and show yourself!" she yelled to the spirit. "Come out!"

But the spirit stayed hidden. That was the last time that Laura ignored her instincts. She never forgot that angry spirit and she never saw him again either, not on any of her other visits to the OSR. But every time she looks at her own knee, she can remember that night. The scar still lingers.

Psychic Debra Robinson also knew not to ignore her instincts. She often senses when ghosts and spirits are near. Her chest feels heavy. She grows breathless. Her skin crawls with goosebumps. At the OSR, sometimes these feelings overwhelmed her as she moved through spots where spirits collected. On the staircases going up from the lobby at the OSR, she often felt that she had to push through the spirits, there were so many crowded together. Debra would make her way up to the most remote regions of the deserted prison. There, she would see shadows dancing across the walls that had no relation to the objects in the room. She would hear shufflings and scufflings when no one else was around.

Something—many somethings—were there, Debra often sensed, and she would press against a wall. She didn't want to leave her back exposed.

Once, something reached out and touched the top of Debra's head. It felt like a large hand. And not a friendly hand. Debra knew it was time to leave before anything else happened.

Dianne Weinmann is a medium and has sensed the pain and anger in the ghosts at the OSR—in her own body. Diane took a tour of the prison in 2008. The tour group made their way up to a cell block with several levels. A metal railing divided the cells from the long drop to the concrete floor below. As Diane walked along the hall, pain suddenly shot through her abdomen. It was as if she were being cut in half. Diane doubled over, grabbing her stomach.

As she hid her discomfort, Dianne asked the tour guide if anything had happened in this spot. He explained that this was the spot where an inmate was thrown over the railing and fell to his death.

Later, Dianne was listening to the guide as the group gathered in a room that served as the library. She stood quietly with the

The library at the Ohio State Reformatory

others, taking in the history the guide was explaining. Then it happened again—this time there was a sharp, pinching pain in her arm as if someone was stabbing her with a hypodermic needle.

Dianne asked the guide if the room had served as something else, back when the OSR was open. "This place?" the guide replied. "It used to be the infirmary." Many operations and other medical procedures had been carried out in this space. And although the infirmary was long gone, the spirits that inhabited it were not.

The Ohio State Reformatory still stands today, looming tall over the Ohio cornfields. It is slowly crumbling, trying to return back to the earth. But people work hard every year to shore up the damp plaster walls and replace the crumbling mortar between the bricks. The Mansfield Reformatory Preservation Society raised enough money to put on a new roof. Society members have maintained the warden's apartment, the hallways, and the guard room. They 've added a new courtyard and landscaping. There's even an office, a lounge for volunteers, and a museum. A visitor might almost mistake the OSR for any pleasant, educational historical site.

But it's not. The redbrick building is a reminder of the suffering that took place within its walls. Men lived and died on that ground. They made friends and committed murder. They laughed and screamed. They worked and longed for release. And when they died in the OSR, they didn't always leave. They lingered.

Every year, visitors flood the prison corridors, searching for these spirits. They reach out with monitors, devices, and recorders. Sometimes they see things. Sometimes they hear things. Sometimes

they just sense the presence of the OSR's spirits. But they'll never know all the ghosts that walk the halls and cells. The OSR holds its stories close. It holds its mysteries even closer.

Conclusion

Several paranormal-themed TV shows have been filmed at the OSR over the years, including *Ghost Adventures*, *100 Things to Do Before You Die*, and *Most Terrifying Places in America*. Music videos have been filmed on the grounds, and major motion pictures, including *Shawshank Redemption*, have used the OSR as a location.

The Mansfield Reformatory Preservation Society was formed in 1992. Its mission was to turn the prison into a museum and conduct tours to help fund grounds rehabilitation projects, and it currently works to stabilize the buildings against further deterioration. And it has done a good job, because more than 120,000 guests visit every year.

The history of the OSR is still being made and will continue to be made as long as the people want to visit the place and take in this impressive structure and walk through the halls, cell blocks, and grounds. History lovers and paranormal investigators alike will continue to come and visit. And what about the shadowy forms, eerie apparitions, and ghostly shapes that lurk inside? As Edgar Allan Poe said, "The boundaries which divide Life from Death are at best shadowy and vague. Who shall say where the one ends, and where the other begins?"

So if you have a chance to visit the Ohio State Reformatory in Mansfield, we hope you have an experience that will help you form an answer to Mr. Poe's question . . .